D1683266

FEB 1 6 2016

WOODS BRANCH
GROSSE POINTE PUBLIC LIBRARY
GROSSE POINTE, MI 48236

Learning to Read, Step by Step!

Ready to Read Preschool–Kindergarten
• big type and easy words • rhyme and rhythm • picture clues
For children who know the alphabet and are eager to begin reading.

Reading with Help Preschool–Grade 1
• basic vocabulary • short sentences • simple stories
For children who recognize familiar words and sound out new words with help.

Reading on Your Own Grades 1–3
• engaging characters • easy-to-follow plots • popular topics
For children who are ready to read on their own.

Reading Paragraphs Grades 2–3
• challenging vocabulary • short paragraphs • exciting stories
For newly independent readers who read simple sentences with confidence.

Ready for Chapters Grades 2–4
• chapters • longer paragraphs • full-color art
For children who want to take the plunge into chapter books but still like colorful pictures.

STEP INTO READING® is designed to give every child a successful reading experience. The grade levels are only guides; children will progress through the steps at their own speed, developing confidence in their reading. The F&P Text Level on the back cover serves as another tool to help you choose the right book for your child.

Remember, a lifetime love of reading starts with a single step!

For my main little man, Charlie K. —K.K.

We have made every effort to trace the ownership of all copyrighted material and to secure permission from copyright holders. In the event of future questions arising as to the use of any material, we will be pleased to make all necessary corrections in subsequent printings.

Original illustrations by Dr. Seuss appear on the following pages: front cover, 3, 4–5, 9, 13, 16, 18–19, 23, 32, 34–35, 38, 41, 44–45, 47, 48.

Dr. Seuss illustration credits: **Cover** (clockwise from top left): "Noisiest Potty" sketch by Ted (March 17, 1985); *Life* 95, no. 2476 (April 18, 1930), 32; "The Log of the Good Ship" (August 1947); *Spelling Bees: The Oldest and the Newest Rage* (Frederick A. Stokes Company, 1937), 29; San Diego Museum of Art, *Dr. Seuss from Then to Now* (Random House, 1986), 14; *PM* 3, no. 130 (November 16, 1942), 13; *Liberty* 15, no. 20 (May 14, 1938). **Page 3** (clockwise from top left): *Liberty* 15, no. 20 (May 14, 1938); "The Log of the Good Ship" (August 1947); Dr. Seuss, *Horton Hatches the Egg* (Random House, 1940), 55. **Pages 4–5:** Dr. Seuss, *The Butter Battle Book* (Random House, 1984), 13, 28–29, 30–31. **Page 9:** *Spelling Bees: The Oldest and the Newest Rage* (Frederick A. Stokes Company, 1937), 29. **Page 13:** all images from *Jack-O-Lantern* 16, no. 3 (November 26, 1923), 24–25. **Page 16:** *Life* 95, no. 2479 (May 9, 1930), 31. **Page 18** (top to bottom): Essolube newspaper advertisement, "Foil the Zero-doccus!" (December 1932); *Life* 95, no. 2479 (May 9, 1930), 31. **Page 19** (clockwise from top left): "Foiled by Essolube" puzzle bag (detail) (1932); *Secrets of the Deep, Vol. II* (July 1936), 32; Essolube poster card, "Foil the Karbo-nockus!" (January 1933); *Secrets of the Deep, Vol. II* (July 1936), 25. **Page 23:** Dr. Seuss, *Horton Hatches the Egg* (Random House, 1940), 17, 40–41, 54–55. **Page 32:** Dr. Seuss, *Horton Hears a Who!* (Random House, 1954), 16–17. **Pages 34–35:** Dr. Seuss, *The Cat in the Hat* (Random House, 1957), cover. **Page 38:** Dr. Seuss, *If I Ran the Circus* (Random House, 1956), 24–25, 32–33. **Page 41:** Dr. Seuss, *The Foot Book* (Random House, 1968), 19. **Pages 44–45:** Dr. Seuss, *The Butter Battle Book* (Random House, 1984), 28–29, 30–31. **Page 47:** Dr. Seuss, *Oh, the Places You'll Go!* (Random House, 1990), cover. **Page 48:** Dr. Seuss, *The Sneetches and Other Stories* (Random House, 1961), cover; Dr. Seuss, *The Cat in the Hat* (Random House, 1957), cover; Dr. Seuss, *The Lorax* (Random House, 1971), cover.

Dr. Seuss properties TM & © by Dr. Seuss Enterprises, L.P. 2016. All Rights Reserved.

Text copyright © 2016 by Kate Klimo
Cover art and interior illustrations copyright © 2016 by Steve Johnson and Lou Fancher

All rights reserved. Published in the United States by Random House Children's Books, a division of Penguin Random House LLC, New York.

Step into Reading, Random House, and the Random House colophon are registered trademarks of Penguin Random House LLC.

Visit us on the Web!
StepIntoReading.com
randomhousekids.com

Educators and librarians, for a variety of teaching tools, visit us at RHTeachersLibrarians.com

Library of Congress Cataloging-in-Publication Data
Klimo, Kate.
Dr. Seuss : the great doodler / Kate Klimo ; illustrators, Steve Johnson & Lou Fancher.
   pages cm. — (Step into reading. Step 3)
Summary: "How Ted Geisel became Dr. Seuss" —Provided by publisher.
ISBN 978-0-553-49760-1 (trade) — ISBN 978-0-375-97376-5 (lib. bdg.)
ISBN 978-1-101-93551-4 (hardcover) — ISBN 978-0-553-49761-8 (ebook)
1. Seuss, Dr.—Juvenile literature. 2. Authors, American—20th century—Biography—Juvenile literature.
3. Artists—United States—Biography—Juvenile literature. I. Johnson, Steve, 1960– illustrator. II. Title.
PS3513.E2Z688 2015   813'.52—dc23   [B]   2014003082

Printed in the United States of America   10 9 8 7 6 5 4 3 2 1

This book has been officially leveled by using the F&P Text Level Gradient™ Leveling System.

STEP INTO READING

Dr. Seuss
THE GREAT DOODLER

by Kate Klimo

paintings by
Steve Johnson and Lou Fancher

with illustrations by Dr. Seuss

Random House 🏠 New York

It is a beautiful day
in La Jolla, California.
A writer and artist
is at work in his studio.
The telephone rings.
A reporter is calling
with big news.
The writer has won
a big award for his books.
It is the Pulitzer Prize.
The writer is Ted Geisel,
also known as Dr. Seuss.

Ted nearly falls off his chair.
Is this a joke?
Ted loves playing jokes and pranks,
but he takes his work seriously.
Now the world is doing so, too.
Not bad for a lifelong doodler!

Theodor "Ted" Seuss Geisel
was born on March 2, 1904,
in Springfield, Massachusetts.
His mother's name was
Henrietta Seuss Geisel.
She read to him and
his big sister, Marnie.
She also sang chants
she once used to sell pies
in her parents' shop.

He later said he got
his love of wordplay and reading
from his mother.
Thanks to his father, Theodor,
Ted became interested
in machines.
His father tinkered in his shop
making wacky inventions.
One of them was a
machine that made
arm muscles stronger.

From an early age,
Ted liked to doodle.
He always had a pencil
and a pad at hand.
Near his house was a zoo.
Lying in bed at night,
he could hear
the lions roaring
and the elephants trumpeting.
During the day,
he would go there
and doodle pictures of animals.

Marnie said his animals never looked *quite* like the real ones.

Ted had a happy childhood,
until World War I broke out.
The Geisels were
German American.
Many Americans blamed
the war on Germany.
Kids bullied Ted.
He wanted to prove
he was a true American.

So he joined the Boy Scouts
and sold war bonds.
He was one of the
top ten bond sellers!
Former president
Theodore Roosevelt
came to honor the ten Scouts.
But there was a mix-up,
and no medal for Ted.
He was so embarrassed!
Ever since that day,
he had stage fright.

After high school,
Ted went to Dartmouth College.
He worked on
the humor magazine.
He drew zany-looking
animals with zany names.
A Blvgk was a critter
with an umbrella tail.
Sometimes he signed
his drawings with
just his middle name:
Seuss.

Ted went on to study
at Oxford University in
England.
He was bored by
the long classes,
so he doodled.
A fellow American student
saw him doodling.
"That's a very fine flying cow,"
said Helen Palmer.

"You ought to be an artist."
Ted and Helen
rode around together
on a motorcycle.
Ted wanted to marry Helen.
But how would he
earn a living?

Back in Springfield,

Ted drew tons of cartoons.

He sent them to magazines,

signed Dr. Theophrastus Seuss.

A magazine called

the *Saturday Evening Post*

bought some of his cartoons!

Ted also got a job

at a different magazine.

Now he could marry Helen!

They moved into an apartment

in New York City.

He kept on doodling.

Ted drew a
clever cartoon about
a bug spray called Flit.
The bug-spray company
loved it and gave him
more work.

He became an ad man!
As he did when he was a kid,
he made up zany critters,
this time for ads.
Years later,
zany fish like these would
fill his book *McElligot's Pool.*

Ted wanted
to do more
with his doodling.
A trip
by ocean liner
inspired him.

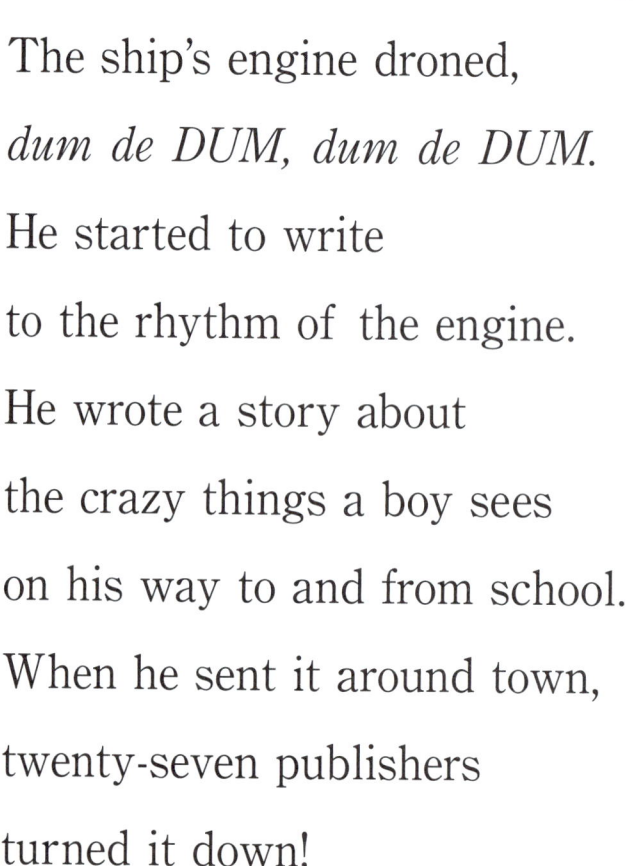

The ship's engine droned,
dum de DUM, dum de DUM.
He started to write
to the rhythm of the engine.
He wrote a story about
the crazy things a boy sees
on his way to and from school.
When he sent it around town,
twenty-seven publishers
turned it down!

Then he ran into a friend
who had just become
a children's book editor.
Mike McClintock
loved the book.
The title was
*And to Think That I Saw It
on Mulberry Street.*
It was Dr. Seuss's
very first book!

Dr. Seuss went on to publish
new children's books
at a steady rate
for the rest of his life.
Some of them won awards.
Horton Hatches the Egg
was a big hit in 1940.
The story was silly,
but it had a deep message.
People loved the elephant
who said,
"I meant what I said
and I said what I meant. . . .
An elephant's faithful
one hundred per cent!"

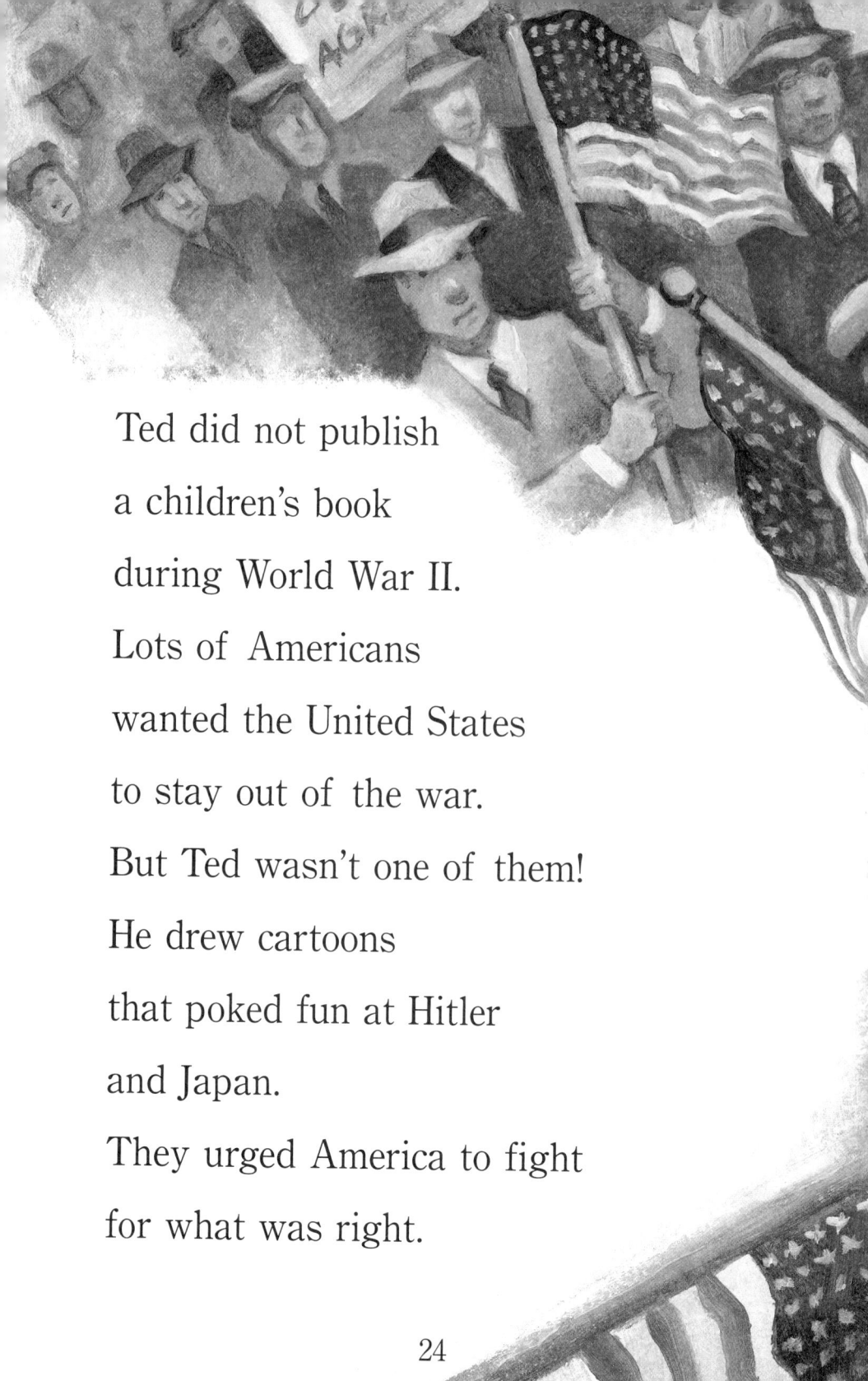

Ted did not publish
a children's book
during World War II.
Lots of Americans
wanted the United States
to stay out of the war.
But Ted wasn't one of them!
He drew cartoons
that poked fun at Hitler
and Japan.
They urged America to fight
for what was right.

America finally entered the war.
Ted joined the army.
He worked with a
team of film makers
in Hollywood.
They made funny training cartoons
starring a soldier
who couldn't do anything right.
Army pals,
like Chuck Jones
and P. D. Eastman,
would work with Ted
in years to come.

After the war,
Ted and Helen stayed
in California.
In 1947,
Ted found
an old,
unused fire tower
in La Jolla.
He and Helen
fell in love with it.
They bought the tower
and made it
their home.

Ted's studio

was in the tower.

He kept a hat rack there

filled with wacky hats:

a fireman's hat from Ecuador,

a Turkish fez,

and admirals' hats

from around the world.

Sometimes,

when he was having trouble

with a story,

he would put on a silly hat.

Ted wanted each book
to be perfect.
He wrote and re-wrote.
He read aloud to Helen.
He sketched and re-sketched.
He pinned his sketches
to a corkboard.

He worked until the words
and pictures were just right.
Then he took his book
to New York City.
In his publisher's office,
he would read it aloud.
Workers would crowd around
to listen to Ted's latest story.

In 1955,
Life magazine ran an article
that said most
early-reading books
were boring.
The job of writing books
for early readers
should go to artists like
Dr. Seuss and Walt Disney.

Ted was dared
to write a book
using 225 simple words.
He thought he could
write the book in two weeks.
It took him more than a year!
The Cat in the Hat
was published in 1957.
The book sold like hotcakes.
It changed the way children
learned how to read.

How the Grinch Stole Christmas!
also came out in 1957.
Someone once said that
the Cat was Ted on a good day
and the Grinch was
Ted on a bad day.
Ted felt he was more like
the gruff and grumpy character.
His car's license plate
even said *Grinch*.

Eight years later,
Ted worked with Chuck Jones
to make an animated
television special based on
*How the Grinch
Stole Christmas!*
Both the show
and the book became
Christmas classics.

In 1958, Ted became

president of Beginner Books.

He would publish

a line of easy-to-read books

like *The Cat in the Hat*.

The office was like a fun house!

Ted wrote some of the readers.

His wife, Helen,

wrote some, too.

He hired friends to do others.

Mike McClintock wrote

A Fly Went By.

P. D. Eastman wrote *Go, Dog. Go!*

Ted published

Stan and Jan Berenstain's

first books about

the Berenstain Bears.

Everything Ted touched
turned into a bestseller.
Then, in 1967,
a terrible thing happened.
Helen died.
Ted was lonely and lost!

A year later,
he married
Audrey Stone Dimond.
She had a good eye.
She wanted Ted to use
more color in his books.
Ted's work became
more colorful.

Audrey came to live
with Ted in the tower.
From there,
he saw how much construction
was taking place.
Trees came down
and buildings went up.
So he started doodling about it.
He wrote *The Lorax*.

It is the story of a little creature
who speaks for the trees.
He tries to save them
from the greedy Once-ler.
The story carried
a powerful message
about our
environment.

Another book with a
powerful message
was *The Butter Battle Book.*
It tells about
the Yooks and the Zooks.
Their two armies are fighting
over which side
of their bread to butter.
The fight is silly,
but their weapons are serious.

Will deadly bombs be dropped?
The story never says.
Some people felt the book
was too scary for children.
But Ted knew
kids could handle it.
He felt his message,
about the madness of
nuclear war,
was important.

Ted was now world-famous.
For some years,
he had been sick with cancer.
But there was one more
book he needed to write.
It was a book of advice
about life's ups and downs
called *Oh, the Places You'll Go!*

"So be sure when you step.
  Step with care and great tact
  and remember that Life's
  a Great Balancing Act. . . .
  And will you succeed?
  Yes! You will, indeed!
  (98 and ¾ percent guaranteed.)
  KID, YOU'LL MOVE MOUNTAINS!"

In a way,
these were Ted's
parting words.
He died on
September 24, 1991.
He left behind forty-four books
that have brought
millions of children
a great deal of joy.

Every spring
on Ted's birthday,
people get together.
They wear the striped Cat hat.
And they celebrate
the words, the pictures,
and the spirit
of Dr. Seuss,
the Great Doodler.